AF375503

WHAT HAPPENS DURING WAR CRIME TRIALS?

HISTORY BOOK 6TH GRADE CHILDREN'S HISTORY BOOKS

Horrible things happen during wars. But in the last hundred years the concept of "war crimes" has been created which means soldiers or government leaders can be punished for what they did or ordered during a war. Let's find out how this works.

THE IDEA OF A "WAR CRIME"

Calling a thing a "war crime" comes from the idea that people can be held responsible for their bad actions, even if they were acting during a crisis. A soldier who kills civilians, and the general or political leader who orders that murder, can all be called to account.

Nations have agreed that war crimes, and crimes against humanity in general, are among the most serious crimes that international legal bodies can deal with. There is no "statute of limitations" on prosecuting the person who committed such a crime. That is, even if the crime was committed thirty years ago, in a war mostly forgotten, the person who caused the crime can be brought to trial.

GAVEL IN COURT ROOM

U.S. FIELD HOSPITAL

Before World War II, there was little concept of a "war crime". There were informal agreements, for instance that armies would not attack hospitals of the other army, but those agreements were often ignored. People assumed that war was horrible, not just for the soldiers with weapons in their hands, but for any civilians, even children, who got in the way.

In earlier times, the winning side in a war might punish a soldier or leader of the other country's army for horrible deeds, if they could catch him, but there was no agreement that even losing generals or their soldiers should be punished for what they had done.

THEMIS GODDESS OF JUSTICE

CHINESE KILLED BY JAPANESE ARMY

Nations began developing a new idea about war crimes during World War II, 1939-45. It became obvious that both Germany and Japan were responsible for horrible events that caused the deaths of millions of people who could not fight back (read who was involved in World War II in the Baby Professor book *The Allied Powers vs. the Axis Powers in World War II*).

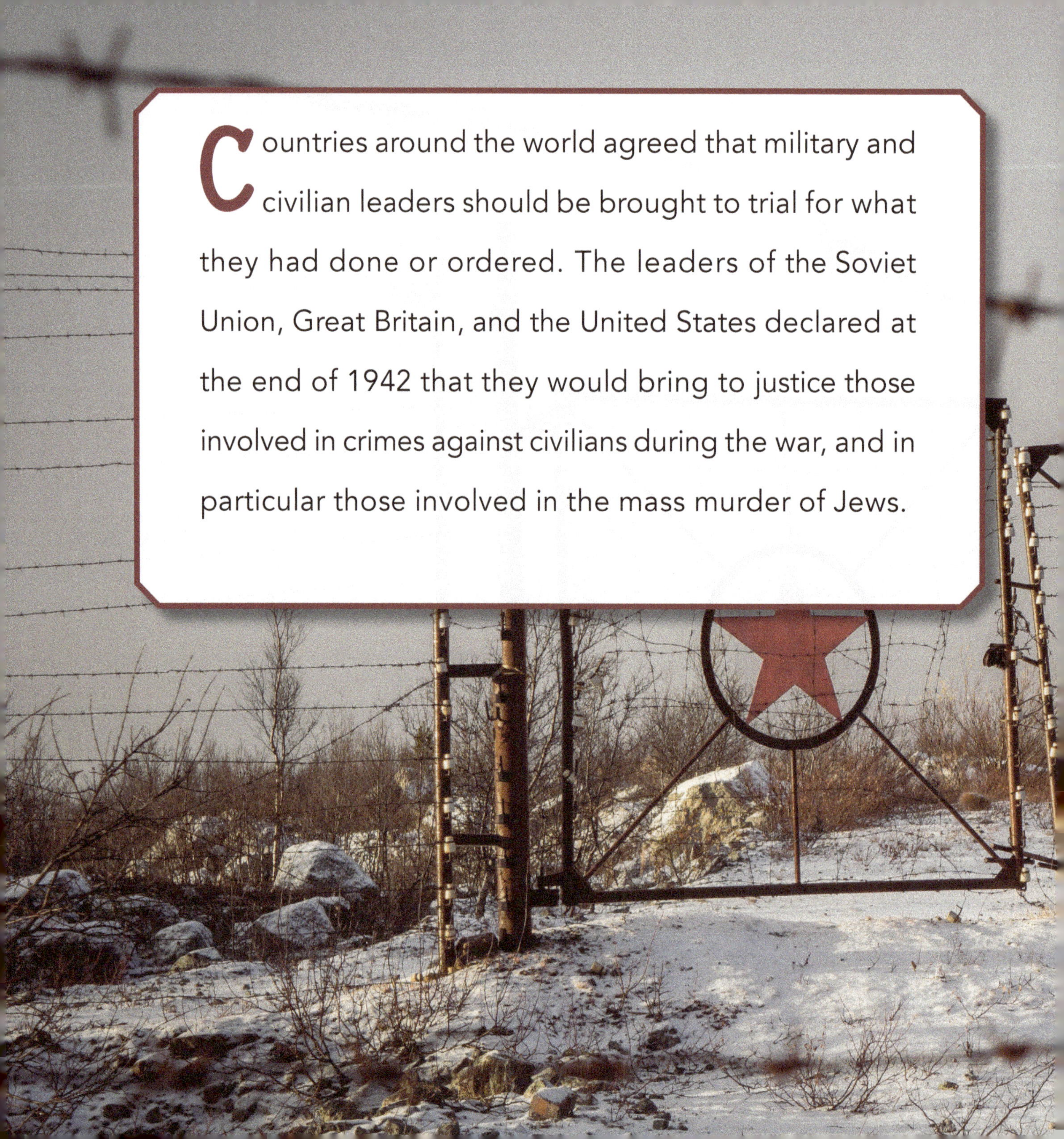
Countries around the world agreed that military and civilian leaders should be brought to trial for what they had done or ordered. The leaders of the Soviet Union, Great Britain, and the United States declared at the end of 1942 that they would bring to justice those involved in crimes against civilians during the war, and in particular those involved in the mass murder of Jews.

SOVIET UNION BORDER

THE HAGUE (INTERNATIONAL CRIMINAL TRIBUNAL BUILDING)

The War Crimes Tribunals held after the end of World War II form the model for all future trials of people who may have committed crimes against humanity. Unfortunately, horrible acts keep going on, and war crimes trials keep needing to be held.

WHAT WAR CRIMES ARE LIKE

An agreement called the Geneva Convention defines what acts are war crimes. Most of the nations of the world have signed the Geneva Convention and have agreed that its citizens can be judged by it.

The Geneva Convention defines general types of war crimes:

FIRST GENEVA CONVENTION

TRIAL AT NUREMBERG

CRIMES AGAINST PEACE

These are acts to plan, prepare for, start, or carry out a war of aggression, or a war that violates international treaties and promises.

VIOLATIONS OF THE "CUSTOMS OF WAR"

Even in ancient times there were ideas about what sort of thing was permitted (killing the person who is trying to kill you) and not permitted (killing babies in an orphanage) even in the heat of war. These violations include actions like:

- Torturing or murdering prisoners, or forcing them to perform slave labor.

- Killing hostages.

MISTREATED PRISONERS

- Using captured soldiers or prisoners for inhuman treatment, including using them as experimental subjects without their agreement.

- Stealing or destroying private property.

- Destroying whole cities, towns, or villages for no military purpose.

DESTROYED CITY IN LONDON

MASS EXECUTION OF ALL THE MEN
IN LIDICE, CZECHOSLOVAKIA

These crimes also include acts against a whole population for no military purpose, like:

- Mass murder or torture.

- Enslavement.

- Deporting whole peoples from their homeland to some other place without their agreement.

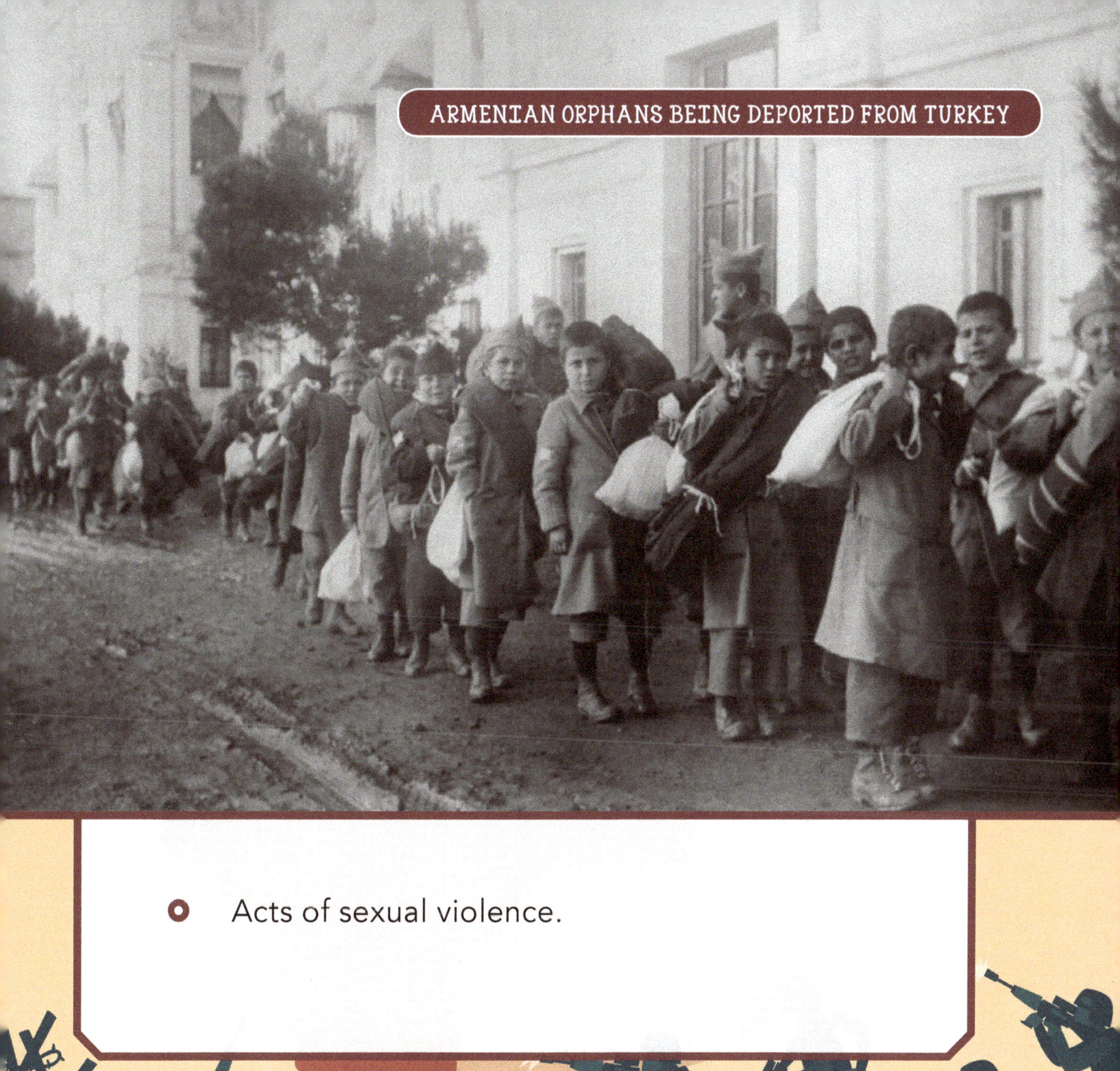

- Acts of sexual violence.

THE YOUTH HOLDING THE PHOTOS OF
VICTIMS OF THE 1992 KHOJALY GENOCIDE

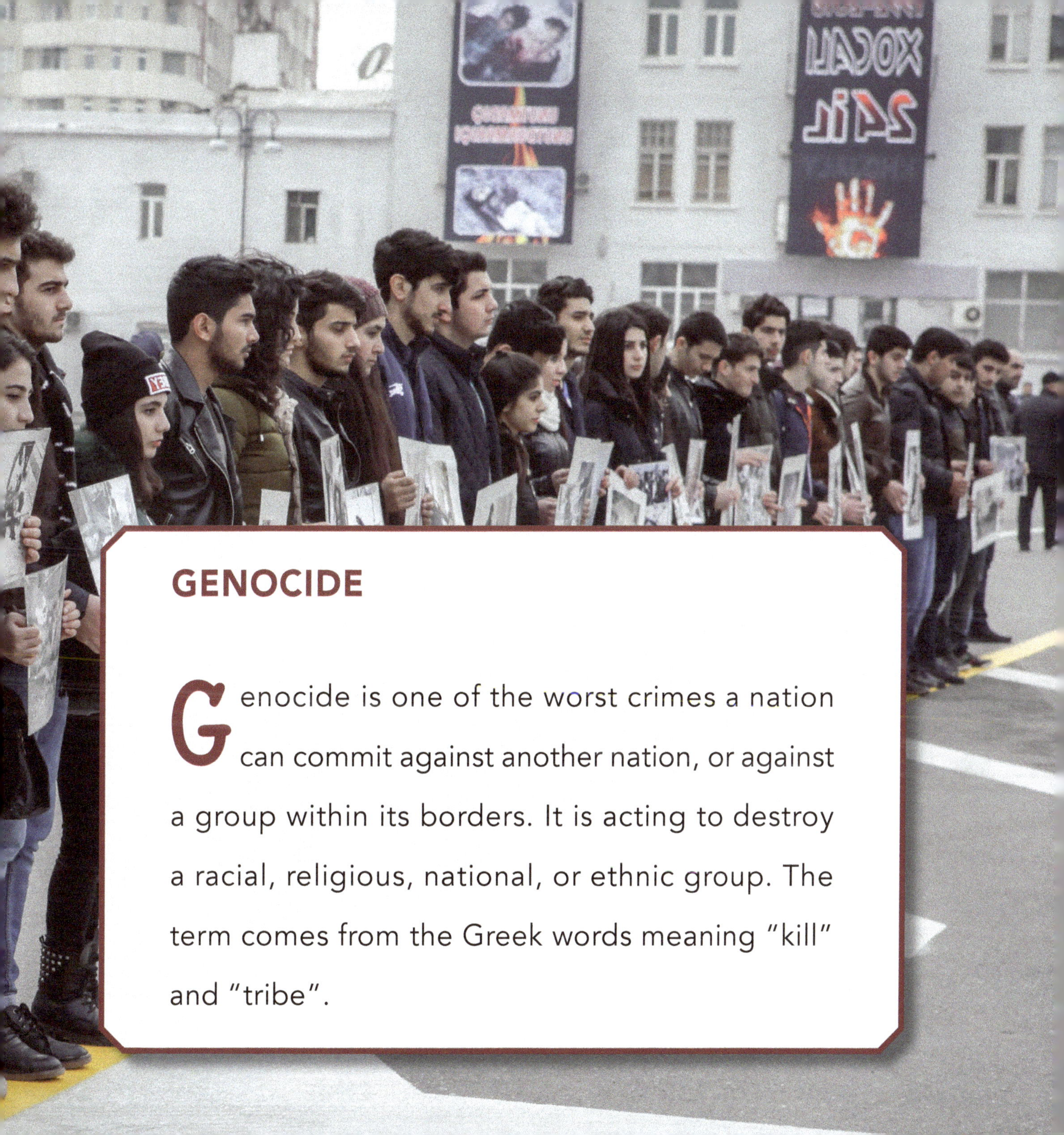

GENOCIDE

Genocide is one of the worst crimes a nation can commit against another nation, or against a group within its borders. It is acting to destroy a racial, religious, national, or ethnic group. The term comes from the Greek words meaning "kill" and "tribe".

Before and during World War II, Germany followed an energetic policy of genocide against peoples its leaders found unacceptable. Target groups included Jews, of whom more than six million were executed in death camps during the war, Gypsies (or "Romany", a stateless people from eastern Europe), homosexuals, and other "deviants".

DEAD PRISONERS IN NAZI CONCENTRATION CAMPS

UNITED NATIONS
NATIONS UNIES
NATIONAL CONVENTION

Based on the evidence of the war crimes trials after World War II, and what Allied troops saw and learned as they liberated the death camps, the United Nations adopted the Convention on Genocide. It establishes genocide as a crime under international law even if it is not seen as a crime within the country where the actions take place. The Geneva Convention says that the people who lead, encourage, order, or approve of such actions can be found just as guilty as the people who commit them.

FOLLOWING ORDERS

In war crimes trials, defendants often say, "I was just following orders. If I had not done this horrible thing, those over me would have killed me." The Geneva Convention says that such a defense, if it can be proved, may reduce the sentence of the person who is found guilty, but it does not excuse them from responsibility for their actions.

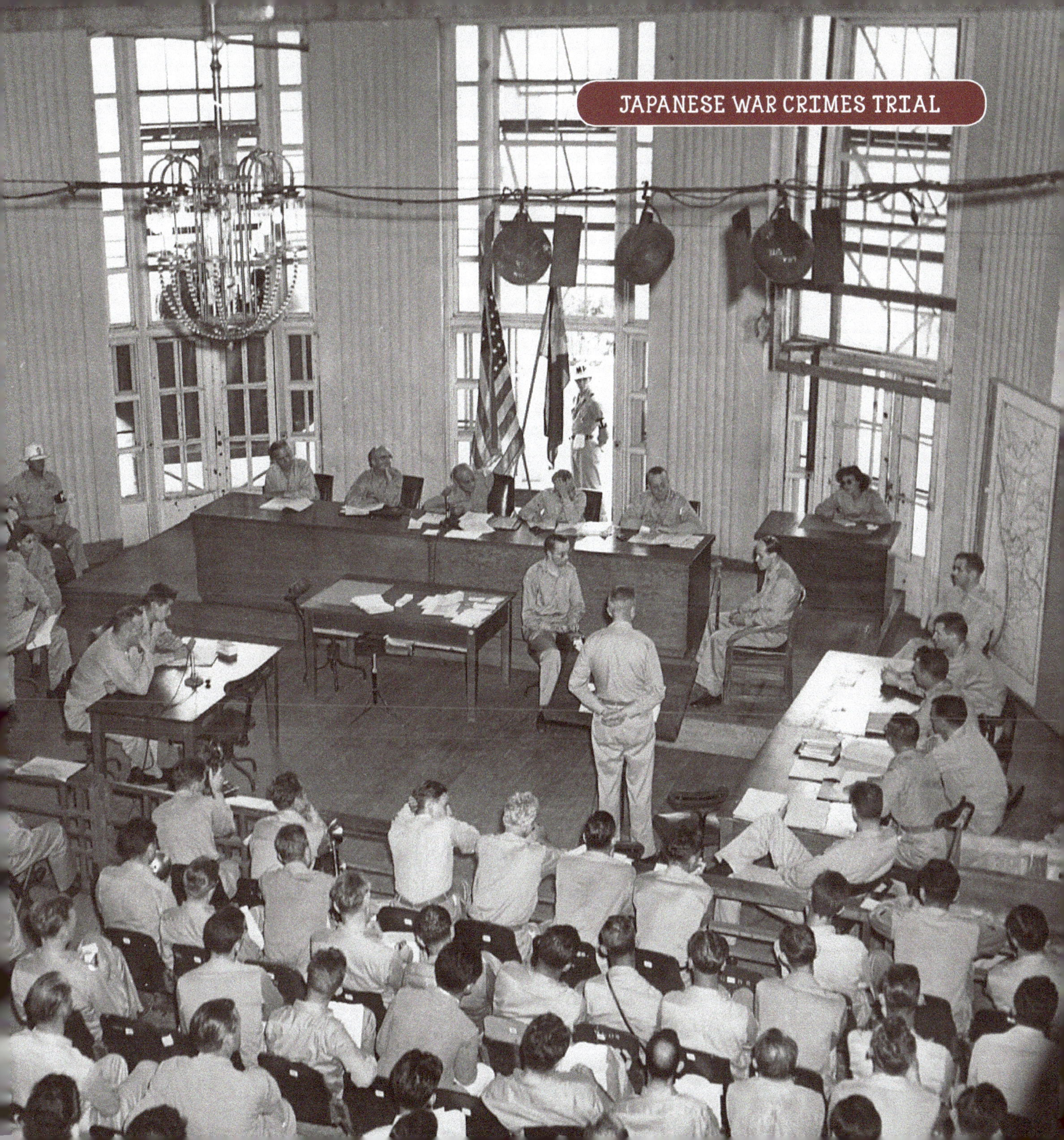
JAPANESE WAR CRIMES TRIAL

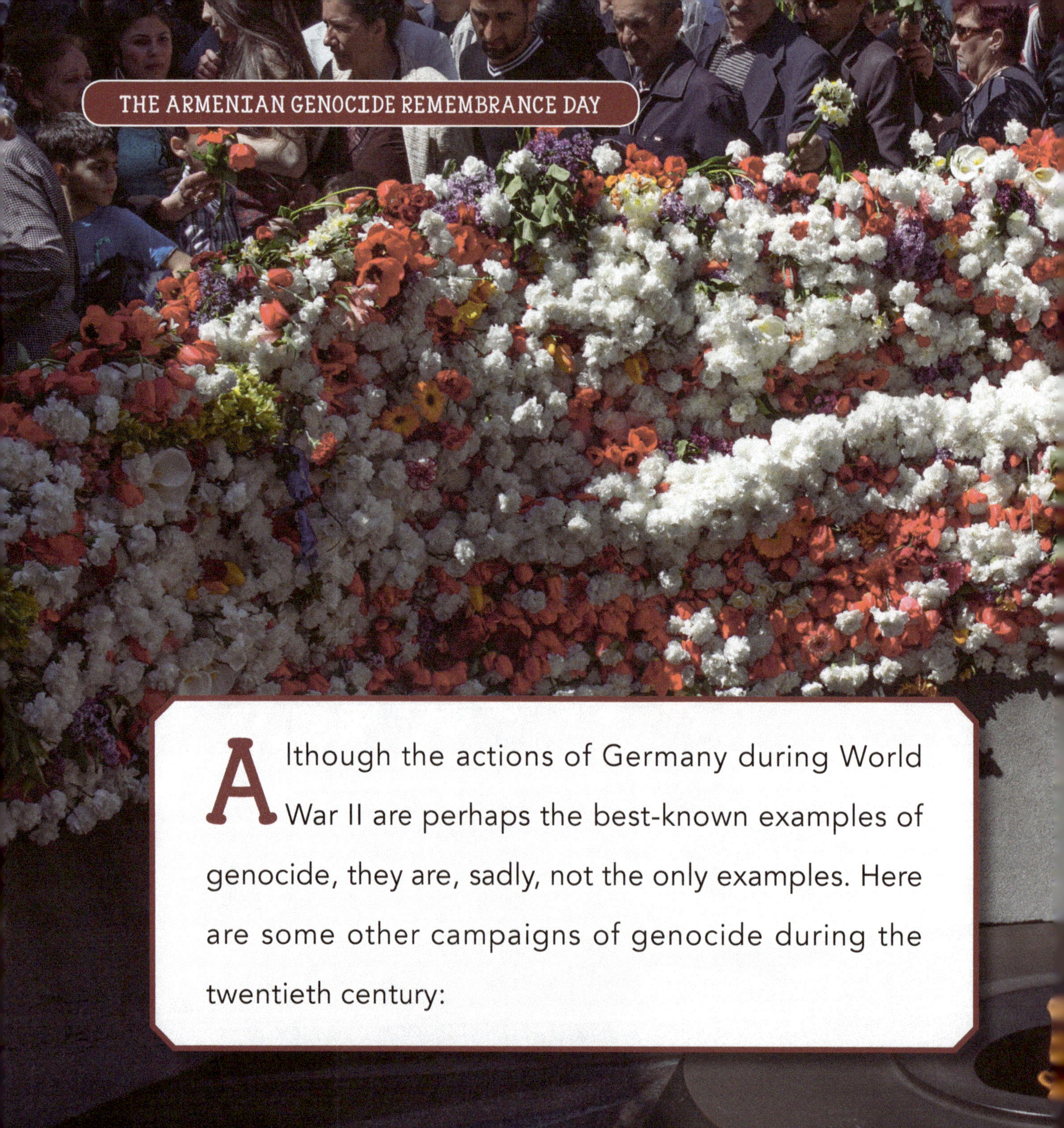

Although the actions of Germany during World War II are perhaps the best-known examples of genocide, they are, sadly, not the only examples. Here are some other campaigns of genocide during the twentieth century:

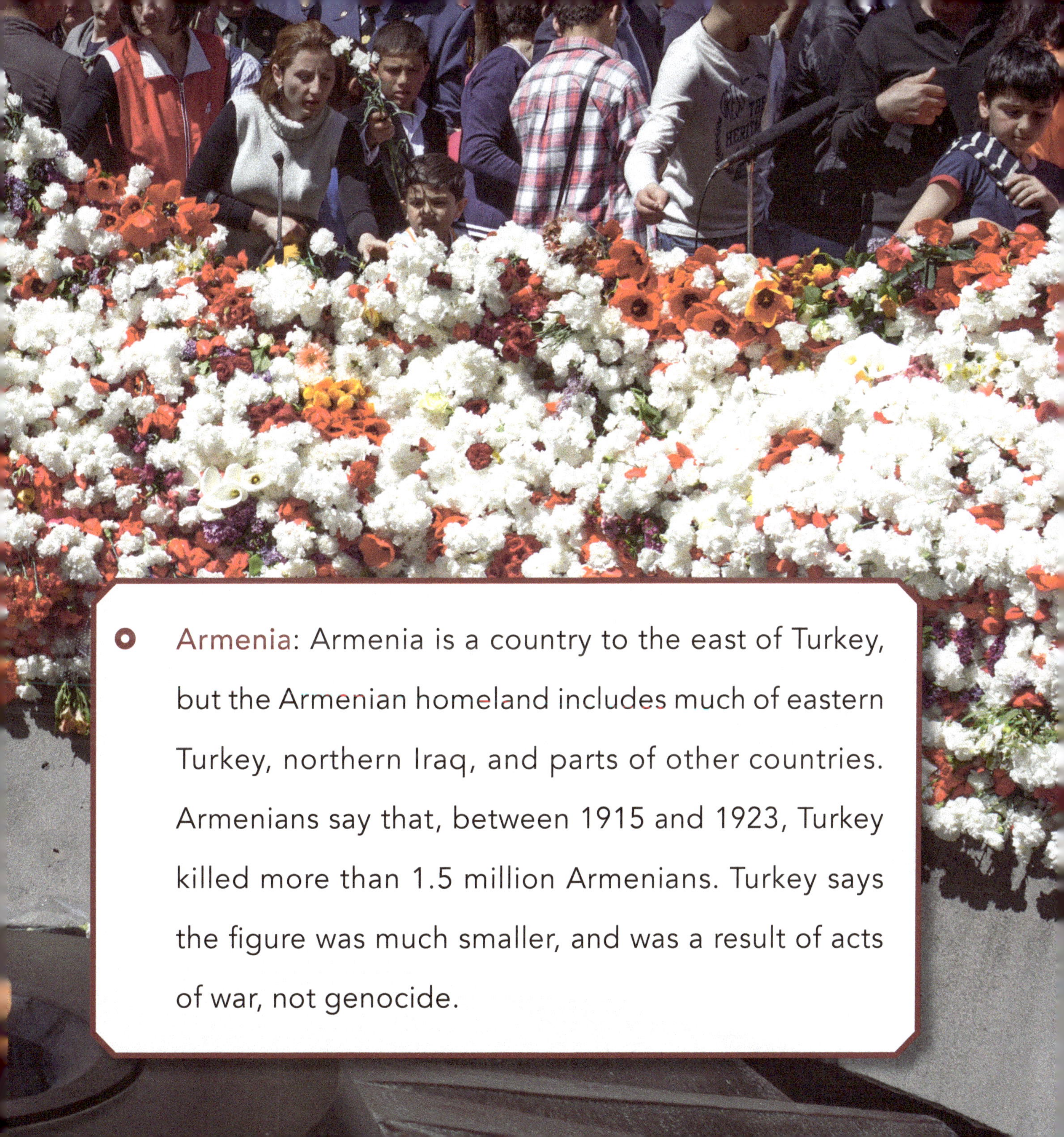

- **Armenia:** Armenia is a country to the east of Turkey, but the Armenian homeland includes much of eastern Turkey, northern Iraq, and parts of other countries. Armenians say that, between 1915 and 1923, Turkey killed more than 1.5 million Armenians. Turkey says the figure was much smaller, and was a result of acts of war, not genocide.

- **Rwanda:** In 1994 the Hutu people of Rwanda in central Africa conducted a campaign to exterminate the Tutsi people of the country. Over 800,000 Tutsis and moderate Hutus were killed, and thousands more became refugees in other countries.

RWANDAN SOLDIERS

MEMORIAL AND CEMETERY FOR THE VICTIMS OF THE MASSACRE

- **The former Yugoslavia**: Yugoslavia was formed after World War II as a grouping of several peoples in the Balkan region of Europe. As the nation started to break apart in the 1990s into smaller countries, Serbian forces conducted acts of genocide against Bosnian communities living in traditionally Serbian territory. More than eight thousand people died.

HOW WAR CRIMES TRIALS OPERATE

Historically, when one army won a battle it often put to death the leaders of the other army. If it conquered another country, it might put to death the leaders of that country. People on the winning side who did horrible things might get medals and promotions. This is known as "winner's justice".

GERMAN WAR CRIMES TRIALS

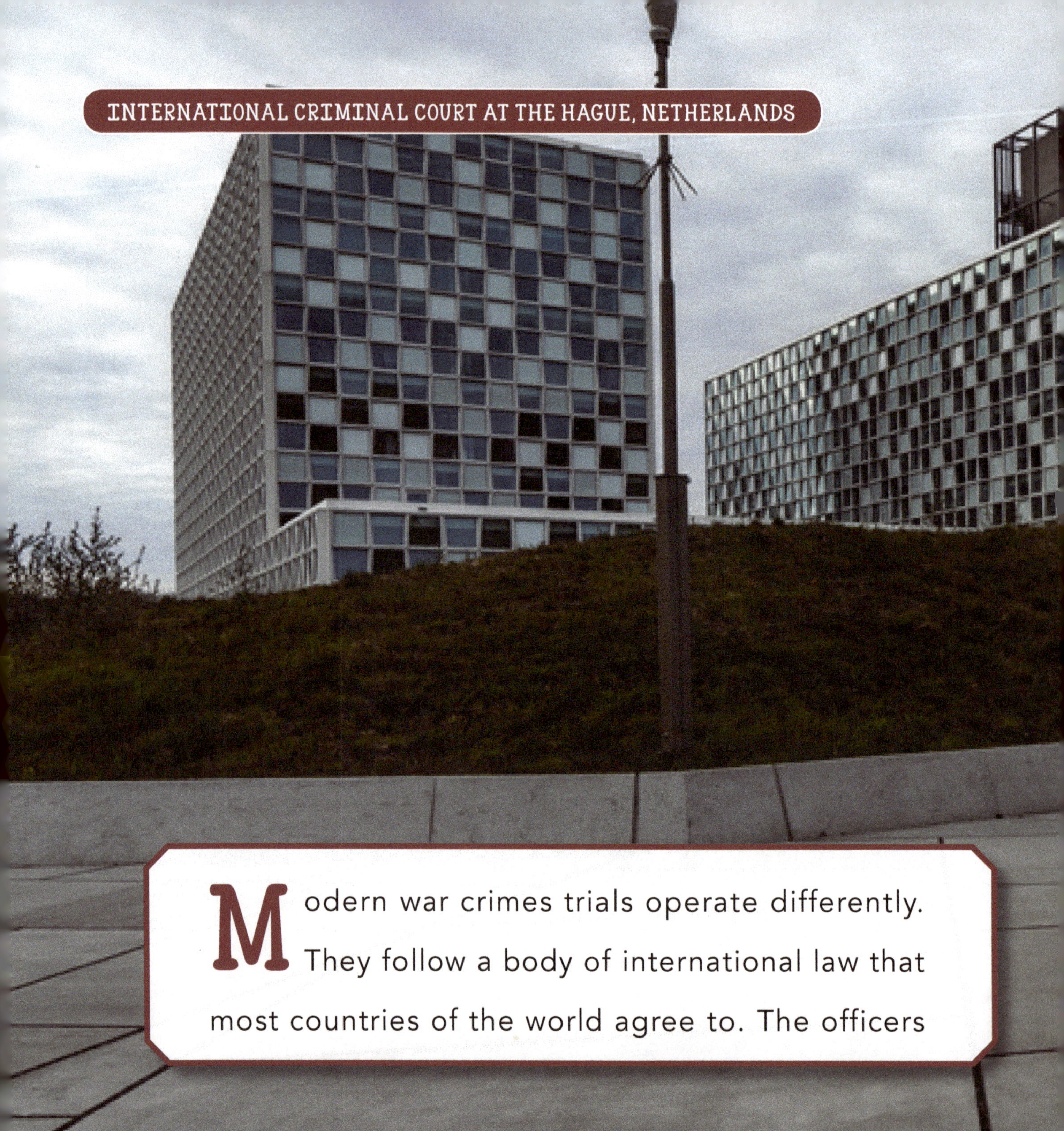

Modern war crimes trials operate differently. They follow a body of international law that most countries of the world agree to. The officers

of the court—the judges, the prosecutors, and other officials—can be from many countries, not just from the country that won the most recent war.

The accused person has a right to legal counsel, to be able to confront his accusers, and to bring evidence in his defense. The prosecution has the burden of proving that the actions took place, and that they violated the Conventions on war crimes. If a person is found guilty, the courts can impose heavy penalties, including imprisonment for a number of years or for the person's lifetime, or immediate execution.

INTERNATIONAL CRIMINAL COURT AT THE HAGUE, NETHERLANDS

PACIFIC OCEAN THEATER OF WORLD WAR II

TRIALS AFTER WORLD WAR II

After World War II there were war crimes trials in both theaters of war, mainly involving military and civilian leaders of Germany and Japan (read about where the war took place in the Baby Professor book *The Theaters of World War II: Europe and the Pacific*).

In Germany, the International Military Tribunal met at Nuremberg, Germany starting in November, 1945, just a few months after the end of the war. Twenty-two senior Nazis (the political party leading Germany during the war) were put on trial, and nineteen were found guilty. Twelve of the guilty were sentenced to death, and the others to terms in prison.

NUREMBERG TRIAL

THE DEFENDANTS AT NUREMBERG TRIALS

From 1946 to 1949 further trials dealt with 177 people, of whom almost 100 were found guilty. These included people who ran or worked in the concentration and death camps, German politicians and industrial leaders, and German lawyers and judges who sent people to their deaths.

In **Japan**, the International Military Tribunal heard cases in Tokyo from early 1946 to late 1948. Twenty-eight people were tried, and twenty-five were found guilty. Two others died during their trial before sentence could be passed, and one was declared not mentally competent.

JAPANESE WAR CRIMES TRIAL

JUSTICE IN A HARD WORLD

People with power often do hard things to people who cannot resist them. They do these things for personal gain, for some belief that leads them to hate the other people, or even just for the "cleansing effect" on a nation. We can never take for granted that these horrible things will not happen again, even in "civilized" countries.

Read Baby Professor books like *Who Was Josef Stalin?*, *The Heart-Shattering Facts about the Trail of Tears*, and *The Wounded Knee Massacre* to learn about acts of genocide in other countries, events for which nobody was punished.

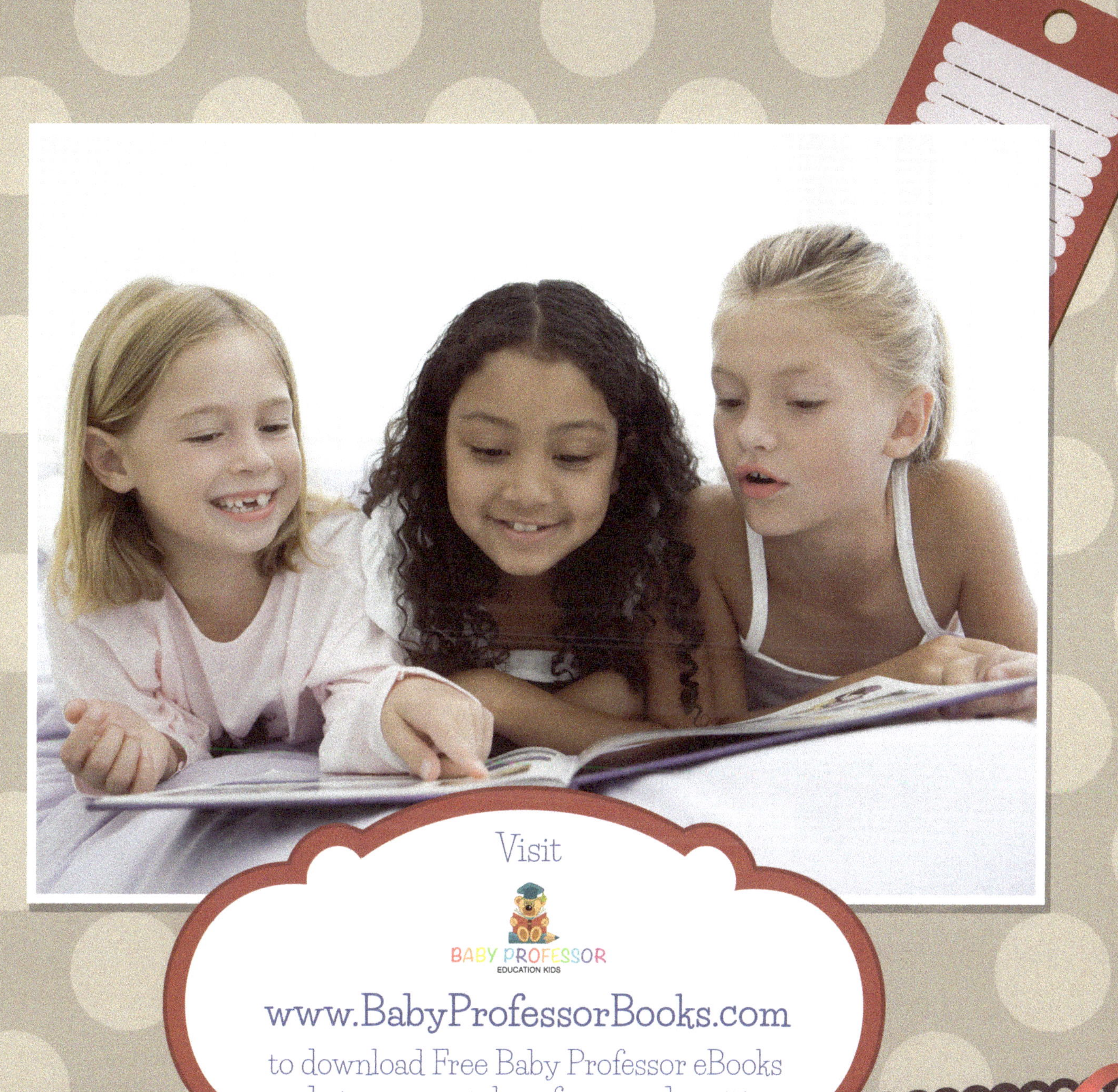
Visit
BABY PROFESSOR
EDUCATION KIDS
www.BabyProfessorBooks.com
to download Free Baby Professor eBooks
and view our catalog of new and exciting
Children's Books